D1564567

BOOKS BY DARYL HINE

RESIDENT ALIEN

695

RESIDENT ALIEN

Poems *by* Daryl Hine

New York   Atheneum   *1975*

ACKNOWLEDGEMENTS: *Linear A* and *Vowel Movements* were first published in *Poetry; Acre* and *A Thousand Words* in *The New Yorker*. Other poems first appeared in *Harpers Magazine, The New American Review, The New Republic, The New York Times, Antaeus, The Unmuzzled Ox, The Tamarack Review, Encounter,* and *Counter Measures*. Three poems appeared in broadside form published, respectively, by The Pomegranate Press, The Unicorn Press, and Pasdeloup Press. *Two Anagrams* are reprinted from *Jiggery-Pokery,* edited by Anthony Hecht and John Hollander, Atheneum, New York, 1967.

Library of Congress catalog card number: 74-19668
ISBN 0-689-106513
Published simultaneously in Canada by McClelland and Stewart Ltd
Manufactured in the United States of America by
Halliday Lithograph Corporation, West Hanover, Massachusetts
Designed by Harry Ford
First Edition

For Samuel Todes

CONTENTS

RESIDENT ALIEN

COMMONPLACES

For Michael Mesic

Places have no memory for faces.
This nowhere landscape like a windy corner,
Not the sort of spot one would have chosen
For a rendezvous, distinct, unpromising,
Metaphysical, featureless, flat, frozen,
Where anyone might feel a foreigner,
Has been somewhere one day none the less.

An accident, perhaps, such as occur
To anybody anywhere like home,
Or a meeting—who cares to recall
Of their first encounter the inauspicious setting?
Everyone, equivocal as we all
Are about sacred places, Mudville, Rome,
Texts whose true reading must remain obscure

And possibly corrupt, a palimpsest
Of names effaced or scarcely legible,
Initials which do not need to be completed,
Transitive four letter verbs that sing.
Thus literature is phrase by phrase deleted
As time decides which words are eligible
For honour, and erases all the rest.

BURNT OUT

For John Miller

To come home at midnight and find everything gone
As if by disenchantment, blackened trash and rubble
In the place of your address, and to have to demand
Of a bystander, a small crowd having gathered
In partial curiosity, "What happened?"
Is one definition of catastrophe—
Though not, for all we know, the ultimate.
Haven't we been threatened with the fire?
You may only be the first to go,
An example of that rhetoric
Which sees in flames an opportunity
To eradicate all wrongs and start afresh.

What was it you said then? What could you add,
Having searched the holocaust and salvaged
Not enough from your former life to fill a hatbox,
Hardly more than a handful of the past?
Half-a-dozen charred but, as chance would have it,
Miraculously legible paperbacks:
A Charmed Life, The Member of the Wedding,
An Introduction to the Game of Go,
The Fire Screen, Fragments of the Pre-Socratics,
Selected Tales of Edgar Allen Poe:
Out of so many why were these few elected?
How do they delineate a point of view?

The point of view of the ruined, which you know
Has been credited with simplicity,
Appears to me impossibly complex.
When one loses everything, is he
Disembarassed, free to be himself,
Or merely impoverished and out of luck?
The *Aeneid* and *Götterdämmerung*
Present the paradox in different ways:

In both a newer, maybe better world
Projected on the ruins of the old;
One, a hero modified by loss,
The other, shapeless gold redeemed from dross.

All your books and all your records burnt,
With all your worldly goods and none of mine,
The remains unrecognizable
Or worse, the works reduced to junk,
Nothing but ashes for your furniture,
And nothing but the stars above your head,
Forgive me if I envy you a little
With the jealousy of someone who has lost
Not things but beings, not property but love,
And believe me when I say, my dear,
That this disaster is nothing like the last
Which will befall you someday after all.

A B. C. DIARY

For Anne and Ken Bradley

Sunday: grammar is the science of relations,
Rites of kind, visits, generations,
Regular, undistinguished, mild,
Such as I expected as a child
When games were interrupted by command,
And I, subjected to the bland
Tyranny of relatives, Who and Which,
With their distrust of the poor and envy of the rich,
Malicious gossip, symptoms, sentiment, scores,
Cursed the company of all verbal bores
And Sunday afternoon. How many years have gone
By, and again I must suppress a yawn
In the face of so much comfortable lack
Of comprehension. Why does one come back?
What have their rights and wrongs got to do with me
Whom absence temporarily set free
To eat and dress and answer or not as I pleased?
Now the demon of conformity has seized
Hold of my shrinking soul—to save, or damn?
It's enough to make me question who I am,
Yet no use asking them, they've no idea,
Though doubtless in their own eyes they appear
Unambiguous as the wedding day which breaks
Over the ubiquitous mountains. The mistakes
We made in childhood label us life-long,
Though some suppose that we went wrong
Originally in being born.
Love, whom virtues with grey hairs adorn,
Gay heart, I know that you think none of this,
Since for you existence is sufficient bliss.
For you the hours unnoticed spread their snares,
Nothing disappoints you, nothing scares,
Not even nothingness, the yawning skull
Of boredom. You discern, in the dull,
Their bright intentions, and hear in the commonplace

6

The inarticulate wisdom of the race,
A reservoir where all may drink their fill.
According to you, this world's a garden still,
Who live indefinitely without stimulants,
Indifferent to providence or chance.

Tuesday my embarrassed sense cannot avoid
The omnipresent titter of the void,
Like a dramatist of the *dix-septième*
For whom love and its antidote were much the same.
In theory I adhere to freedom's side,
In practice to discipline's. "Decide!
Decide!" the compulsory chorus chants,
A chorus composed exclusively of aunts
Who taught me ennui and embarrassment
Like euthanasia were not unkindly meant,
That even when there's nothing left to say
It's essential to say something anyway,
For fear a moment slip in silence by
And silence remind us we must die.
Item: one clock brought back from Switzerland
Whose "Cuckoo!" no one affects to understand
As a comment. Briefly undeceived
By fortune, whom our forefathers believed
A goddess, Fortuna, Tyché, Lady Luck,
Like that sarcastic record we are stuck.
Item, the Czechs, dubiously checked
Not mated, now the recent retrospect
Of liberty starts to fade upon their view.
Violence triumphs in imagination too.
Scanning the headlines' signals of distress
For the next gambit in this ghastly game of chess,
I remark that tyranny works everywhere
Just as long as its victims could care
Less, to which they impassively agree.

Later, confronted by the paradox of free
Verse, I trade my meaning for a rhyme.

Thursday. Unpunctual? No, impervious to time,
Patience is your dominating trait,
An infinite capacity for being late,
Afloat in eternity's fluid
Medium. You nicknamed me The Druid
Because of my regard for trees.
It seems several species make you sneeze,
And you detest monkey puzzles; so do I,
But if I had to live without the sky
Or water, I should not mind as much
As never to see leaves again or touch
Wood. In a wood one feels a presence
In comparison to which bipeds are peasants,
Evolution's riff-raff, without roots.
Trees, having learned to know us by our fruits,
Like defoliation, keep us at a distance.
Ecology is merely coexistence.
Conceivably tree worship must seem odd
To someone whose ancestors invented God
In a landscape the opposite of lush
With no vegetation but the burning bush.
Deserts inform the will how free it is,
While, with their limited woodland deities,
What wonder if the painted nation
Of the North profess predestination?
Hence those mutual antitheses
That in a couple cannot fail to please.
The difference that every man and woman
Boast is what we mostly have in common.
Physically and morally akin,
We seek in one another not a twin
But a transcendental object, something else,

The fascination of, not true or false,
But the equal irreconcilables of taste.
Contemporary values, haste and waste,
Translate the Augustan *Festina lente*.
Parsimony in the midst of plenty
Of the sort that soon may cost the earth
Suggests what our economy were worth.
When there are too many mouths to feed
Already, heartless bigots bid us breed
Until nature, surfeited with clients, cease
Her support. You and I do not increase.

Saturday brings me by a sententious route
To what this satire was to be about:
A homecoming and a marriage.
Far be it from an exile to disparage
Either the end or the beginning
Of that without which life would have no meaning,
But the ceremony was a joke,
And not of the kind perpetuated by folk
Lore. At the reception on the lawn they served,
Once the religious wrongs had been observed
With secular solemnity, at the most
A thimbleful of homemade wine to toast
The bride in; tea and coffee were passed later
By the bridegroom got up like a waiter
Typically in his rented tux.
The crux of these affairs is, no one fucks,
Any more than at a funeral
Mortality is alluded to at all.
Officially you'd not infer the pact
We were there to celebrate, the act
Of darkness, from our fruitcake and confetti.
The facts of life, beautiful not pretty
As my family prefer to make believe,

They hold taboo; they neither joy nor grieve
Overtly, perhaps considering emotion
Poppycock, like the Pacific Ocean,
Certainly an impertinent metaphor,
Which as neighbours they scarcely notice anymore,
So you wonder if they know it's there.
Incredulously, *O que j'aille à la mer!*
Our broad mother, not her narrow daughters,
Strait and inlet, domestic waters
Impregnated by the careless rivers.

Monday, belowdecks an unconscious motive quivers,
Waves slap half-heartedly against the hull;
In our wake a sympathetic gull
Follows like a ghost; vaguely through the mist
Land is apprehended to exist
As vapour condenses on the cabin window.
The horizon drops an innuendo
(So the silent ripples on a pond
Imply an event) concerning the beyond
Which opens overnight within our reach
In the changing shapes of the breakers off Long Beach.
Admiring their continual advance
I grow dizzy, as I do before the dance
I sit out after sunset on the shore:
Stars that I have never seen before
Wink at me; planets I think I recognize
Return my stare with cold, unblinking eyes.

Wednesday morning: time to mosey back
From the abyss, along the hairy track
That bisects the backbone of Vancouver Island.
The perils that befall us upon dry land
Where the precipice rises and abruptly drops
Amid gorges, torrents, rockslides, mountaintops,

Are enough to take the breath away
Temporarily. Stones seem here to stay,
To judge by their genealogy, in spite
Of erosion, earthquake, dynamite.
Names out of childhood illustrate the journey:
Nanaimo, Qualicum, Comox, Coombs, Alberni,
Mere dots in the overwhelming wilderness
On the map, the forwarding address
Of animals that elsewhere are extinct
Whose failure is intimately linked
To our success.

                    Friday my itinerary
Specifies an early morning ferry
To the mainland and descent of the "Sunshine Coast"
In a shower: hereabouts almost
Three-hundred-and-sixty days of the year it rains.
This euphemism possibly explains
The hypocrisy of beautiful B.C.,
And how between the mountains and the sea
The affluent in glass houses live,
Or why, at seventeen a fugitive
From the elemental West, I sought
Salvation in the East, and found it not
Only enlightening but entertaining.
If it's childish to complain because it's raining
Childhood's an incurable complaint.
But I have learned to appreciate the faint
Deliquescence of the atmosphere,
As of the world dissolving in a tear,
That I find inevitably here.
Confronted by the everlasting rain,
My metaphysical reaction is, Again!
Reincarnation lives! since one survives
In a single life innumerable lives

Wholly or in part significant:
You'd like to understand them, but you can't.

Sunday. Obvious effects have subtle causes,
And the longest effusion ultimately pauses
For breath on the very brink of the absurd,
The future of the line and of the word
Threatened by fundamental incoherence.
Thanks to a spontaneous appearance
Which only premeditation can impart,
An accident owes everything to art.
It's not really unreasonable, is it,
If every time I pay them a visit
My family present me with a bill
Overdue and unreceipted still?
I'll pay it if it kills me, and it will.
Funny, under so much natural beauty
To discern the dull death's head of duty
Fixed in an uncompromising grin!
We resident aliens end where we begin.

SECOND THOUGHTS

How fascinating ordinary life is,
Or used to be! Selected letters tell us
Almost more than we need to know about ourselves.
Slang, the argot of affection, dates
Fatally and soon, till each stale page of gossip
Makes you want to change your name or vomit.
How could I call anybody "doll"?
Commend as "cute"? or condemn as "crummy"?
Words, subjected to prolonged abuse,
Revenge themselves upon the oppressor, strike;
The phrase outraged by vulgar repetition
Returns intact to haunt its ravishers.
Yet, the sentiments were certainly sincere,
For want of a better word, the motives real;
As for the language: let its artless prattle
Not be forgotten as an object lesson
That only the most recherché style, the most affected
Can sustain the weight of time and tears and truth.

A style, that is, where anything may happen:
A sudden, not quite unforeseen conversion,
The misery of one dead-end love affair
Abandoned for another equally one-sided;
Throughout, the occasion for each thundering mistake,
The same unconscious credulity and courage.
But though incident and metaphor abound,
And the margins overflow with characters
Other than the author's, parenthetic glimpses
Of London in August, Easter in the Highlands,
Or New Year's Eve at a station buffet in East Berlin,
Even from the enigmatic postscripts
Any trace of repentance is altogether lacking.

Well, I am young, or at least I was—
As if youth could in itself extenuate

Certain failings of our former selves
Unforgivable because too often funny!
Why fuss about such widespread foolishness
When it is an all but universal fault?
These documents demonstrate if anything
The eternal adolescence of the soul,
Or that everything is mortal except life.
The nonsense that an avatar survives,
Boredom, disappointment, and self-knowledge,
And being silly, giggles still at horrors,
And being human sometimes regrets his mis-spent youth!

THE MAN WHO EDITED *MLLE*   *For Eleanor Perenyi*

Leaves on closely shaven lawns, debilitated, brown,
Are scrupulously swept and bagged, yet more leaves flutter down
Onto that of Mr Wright, to his considerable pleasure,
Since picking up after nature's how he likes to spend the leisure
He wagered for all week, under a naked sky
Daily more conspicuous between the branches. Why
Mr Wright, a man with all the marks of secular success,
An interesting job and a desirable address,
Should want to put on overalls, lean on a rake, and brood
On the deciduous vistas of suburban solitude
May transpire in the sequel. Anyway, he does.
In another incarnation it is possible he was
A peasant, and it may be vegetative memories
Return in Autumn now and again among the unconscious trees.
In the present life our hero is a journalist of sorts,
Not the sort who makes the news and meteorological reports,
But one you're not meant to notice, the ghost behind the scenes
That fill most of the pages of technicolour magazines
Designed simultaneously to titillate and sell;
In short, Mr Wright was the man who edited *Mlle*.

Not that he was effeminate! He couldn't afford that!
He wore a jacket and a tie, he even wore a hat
When he had to. He was married, though they hadn't any young—
Mrs Wright was handsome, vague, and very highly strung.
He had dutifully tasted, like *hors d'oeuvres*, the varied joys
Enjoined by marriage manuals, but his partner's equipoise
Was precarious at best; her heart was just not in sex,
And while this is a situation that proverbially wrecks
Any union, it didn't seem to do the Wrights' much harm:
His heart wasn't in it either, it was with *Glamor*, *Vogue*, and *Charm*.
He loved his work, which is abnormal in an automatic age
Of drudgery, he loved the lay-out and the look of every page,
The colours of the cover and the cover-girls as well,
The subscribers, the contributors, the office personnel,

The masthead, the mystique, the manpower and make-up of *Mlle*.

He caught the 9:15 each morning, (he never learned to drive)
Returning regularly on the 7:45
"To avoid the rush hour traffic", drank martinis-on-the-rocks,
Glanced at The Times at breakfast, had some interest in stocks,
Voted Democrat—or Republican—which, didn't seem to matter,
Gradually was growing bald and inevitably fatter.
In fine, he did as you and I and all good Christians do,
Anglo-Saxon Protestants, which class includes a few
Catholic agnostics and the odd assimilated Jew.
Except in his profession: there he was unique.
He had flair, pizzaz, and know-how, an unparalleled sense of chic.
And what he didn't know about women's fashions and their fads
Was more than compensated for within the full-page ads
That fill out the bulk of *Mlle*, padding that pretty creature's
Figure, till double-spreads obscure some of her finer features,
The book reviews and recipes, short stories and light verse
That explain why women's monthlies are both a blessing and a curse,
Their cultural jam afforded by a backward avant-garde,
While advertisements for underwear provide their bread-and-lard.
Now it's easy to poke fun at publishing and pillory Mad Ave's
Excesses, as the have-nots tend to envy and hate the haves—
"Most critics of society merely wish that they were in it,"
Wrote the editor of *Woman's World*. In much less than a minute,
It's said, when you're dying a lifetime passes before the inner eye:
So in the pages of *Mlle* time and life flash by,
Or something not unlike them, as you drown in opulence,
Furs, foundation garments, status symbols, shoes, and scents,
And above, or beneath all, flesh, alabaster or sun-tanned
The colour of cured leather—but, lest anyone misunderstand,
Mlle was far from being the kind of magazine
The standards of the community would stigmatize obscene,
Its minimal social content and slick commercial spell
Redeeming from indecency the flesh of *Mlle*.

And this flesh was Mr Wright's, to manipulate as he pleased.
Being pulp, the periodical, metaphorically squeezed,
Distilled an elixir like liquified fool's gold,
For the rewards of literature, while infinite, were cold
As the empty nursery upstairs at night when he returned
From work. Thus it was that as the various leaves turned,
And the no less flamboyant folia of the periodical
Flaunted their fall fashions, the change seemed to recall
The truth of that perennial philosophy which teaches
That everything must die. All but abandoned lay the beaches,
The scene of summer's comedy; as if for epilogue
Along the shore a melancholy stroller or stray dog;
Stripped of children and protestors, the parks had now reverted
To their autumnal occupants, the old and the perverted;
The last resorts were forced to close for lack of clientèle,
And decay was evident everywhere, except at *Mlle*.

Or so it seemed at any rate till one night late last Fall
Mr Wright had been awakened by a Correct Wrong Distance call.
He couldn't at first unscramble what the operator said,
Gibberish which might have been a message from the dead
Person-to-person; nonetheless he agreed to accept the charge,
"All pleasant and collect," as they say in Japan. At last at large
As it echoed back from Telestar the voice was faint and shrill.
"Of course I remember you! Good old—is it Bill?
I thought by now you had become a confirmed expatriate.
You're coming to America? This winter? Say, that's great
News! Keep in touch, and we'll get together when you do.
It must be thirty years or more since I, that is, since you . . . "
At a word the Traitors' Gate of memory swung wide
Disgorging his old companion afloat on a flood tide
Of unwanted recollection, the effluvium of youth
Become the sediment of middle age. If spectres speak the truth
As they are rumoured to, this pathetic apparition
Might be capable of blackmail. "You say you're looking for a position

In publishing? Such jobs these days are awfully hard to find,
But what sort of thing, approximately, was it you had in mind?
Anything, provided it's easy and pays pretty well?
I'm afraid there are no openings like that on *Mlle*."

On those who knew him "Bill" had always had the same effect—
The wonder was he called at all, not that he called collect—
Yet one incident struck our editor as worthy of retrospect.
In seventh grade the other had read a book on hypnotism
And proceeded to experiment, by means of a simple prism,
With putting people under. A cooperative victim,
Mr Wright was sorry afterwards that what's-his-name had picked him
But pretended to getting sleepy in the spirit of the joke
And was instructed to remember nothing when he awoke.
The suggestion insinuated then into his nodding head
Was, that before the dawn of his fourteenth birthday he would be dead,
Of what, he had forgotten—perhaps it wasn't specified:
Suffice it to say that daily during the next six months he died,
Afraid to dismiss the prediction as the silly, malicious trick
It was, and by the time the term was over he fell sick
With worry he could not confide for fear of superior laughter.
His indescribable anxiety abated the morning after
His birthday when, alive again, Mr Wright could not believe
His luck or his credulity. As if upon reprieve
The world seemed literally wonderful, till reluctantly it shrank
Back to its usual dull dimensions. And whom did he have to thank
For the whole experience but this importunate mountebank?
Without a word to terminate the plaintive monotone,
In its bedside cradle he replaced the telephone,
And resigned himself half-heartedly once more to righteous slumber,
Resolved to regard the interruption as Mr Wright's Wrong Number,
Proof, if proof were necessary, that the past is hell,
As anyone can see for himself in old issues of *Mlle*.

TWO ANAGRAMS

Li Po

O lip
poli,
I *plo-*
p oil.

Oscar Fingal O'Flahertie Wills Wilde

I? Tried for gain? How scales will fall!
Ill fared till crisis, when awe of gaol,
Law, scared off heart's wing. I lie, I loll,
Wilt. Eros fled so willing a farce. Hail!

CHARM

Charm, against the Undercutter,
Daughter of that ancient dragon,
Sister to the salamander,
Brother to the basilisk,
Son of all that's sinister—
Some mythographers imagine
That Medusa was the mother—
Never gets you anywhere.

Victory is out of question.
Difficult but efficacious
Flight alone from the enchantress
With designs upon your life:
Flight, escape, release, and maybe
Something different, or merely
As a means of locomotion
Through the reaches of the air,

Where, while this is propaganda,
Falling isn't all the matter,
Rather a perpetual
Promise: meeting someone there.
Supernatural her habit
Though her look is all too human.
In the mirror watch her passing
Water, breaking wind, breathe fire.

TACITUS LOQUITUR

On the Death of a Parrot

Fledged amid other scenes at other times,
From branch to branch, from tree to tree I flew,
Fed by such rare or common fruits as grew
Not in your inhospitable climes.

My plumage was more brilliant than the limes
I feasted on; my beak was coral; blue
Was my breast; my eye was bright betimes;
My species, now diminished, always few.

My only natural enemy I knew
At last, his territory time's
Fascinated and apterous crew,
The emperor of all that creeps and climbs.

Tacit I lived, and dying tacit too,
Innocent unless of petty crimes,
I find in these inimitable rhymes
The human tongue with which to talk to you.

EGO LOSS

For S. M. L. Aronson

At a little less than a year and 70 lbs.
A dog named Ego is being retranslated
To fabulous New York from sensible Chicago
    In a laminated case marked Air Freight Cargo
Whose sole aperture is uselessly barred and grated
    Against the barks with which the terminal resounds.

About to be airborne Ego's far from faring well:
    All the air is filled with inarticulate noise;
The minute you turn your back the animal complains.
    His kennel, the regular American cell,
Looks inadequate as home; no wonder he destroys
    It before your eyes: Ego, everywhere in chains.

Psychoanalysis, the feeding of pets teach us
    Before being ourselves we need to eat mother—
Hardly feasible in Ego's hermetic cabin.
    He and I don't have to care for one another
Much in order for mere reality to reach us
    Reciprocally: we make each other happen.

Or else. Ego is unconscious where he is going,
    So incuriosity instead of courage
Surely enables him to prosecute the voyage
    Above the clouds over moribund Lake Erie
In the bowels of a vastly fallible Boeing.
    Already, as Ego audibly grows weary

Of his trip, the forgotten earth comes up to meet him
    As part of his streamlined *descensus Averni*.
Once debarqued at the gate there is Sibyl to greet him.
    In time Ego will awaken from his journey
Disoriented, oblivious of the city
    Where I abide, on the other side of pity.

ON THIS ROCK

Mountains rise above us like ideas
Vague in their superior extent,
Part of the range of disillusionment
Whose arresting outline disappears
Into the circumstantial clouds that look
Like footnotes from above. What wisdom said
The mind has mountains? Imagination read
The history of the world there like a book.

Playing peek-a-boo with famous peaks
Afflicted with the vapours leaves a sense,
Frowned down upon by all that bleak immense
City of rock and ice, that men are freaks,
In the original program of creation,
Afterthoughts. Each jack pine seems a brother;
Even in lichens we perceive another
Example of our own organization,

Tenacious, patient, in a century
Growing perhaps a quarter-of-an-inch:
Glaciers do more daily, an avalanche
In minutes. The eroded immobility
Attributed to mountains is a fable,
Like the Great Divide. They move when you're not looking,
Like stars and stocks, distinctly better looking
From a distance, and chronically unstable.

HAPAX LEGOMENA "To be read, as they were written, once."

For Richard Howard and Sanford Friedman

I *June, 1970*

Stopping shortly in someone else's surroundings, sleeping
Easy between some other body's sleazy cotton sheets,
Imbibing all their instant coffee, cocoa, tea and wine
Innocently (a kind of game—see if you can find it),
Verily eating everything except a maraschino
Cherry lost in the 'fridge, the only animate being
Living still in Ma Belle's hermetically sealed apartment,
Gives one an illusion as of unearned intimacy,
Like peering into strange domestic cells uninvited
At that unguarded spell between first turning on the lights
And what voyeurs like to call Curtains. *Uniusquisque*
Faber suae ipsae fortunae, first, and favourite?
Quotation—familiar, Latin—I found on your strait desk:
Nobody fakes it fortunately, each builds his own nest.

Look, you've feathered yours with given books and pictures paid for,
Cooked and conned by heart: our distinguished, disgruntled Authors
Hold, your list of titles suggests, no mysteries for you,
Though Art has its victims as well as Life. Take Mother Goose
Whose parable of Goldielocks applies curiously
To our situation, temporary intruders here,
Two "sicklified and sentimentalized good girls" sitting
In *your* chair (In a Cathedral there were no where else to sit!)
Drinking your cornucopia, *sopra voce* playing
Cenerentola to your optative Morgan le Fay.
When you return from whatever costly unrewarding
Exotic shore it may be you'll discover what is more
Vestiges of our presence in your absence: a dainty
Impression that will tell you who's been lying in your place?

II *March*, *1972*

Surgam et in mundo vivam—VALERY

Night fidgets into day, gradually
The stricken blind becomes a lambent
Parallelogram—as if it were
Yesterday? Upon the night-stand *Les*
Aides-Mémoires de Madame Truc de Chose
Open, wilted as the *Fleurs du Mal.*
Luck is getting hungry far away.
From your courtyard gurgle, are they doves,
Here, off Manhattan's dynamite row?

We who cannot sleep together lie
Higgledy-piggledy vigilant,
Counting the parachromatical
Strokes till the start of another dull
Functional day; like interior
Decorators, everybody
Prefers just such a neutral décor
To exhibit the furniture with
Which all private studies come equipped.

Who is scratching at the guestroom door?
Max: I hear his asthmatic laugh, and
Figure his horrifying mask, a
Caricature—the friendliest pug
I know—which only goes to show that
Intuition crowns the several
Senses. Different beatific
Visions we can tell by name, but Max
May perceive the beatific smell,

Or taste? or touch? Few have noted down
The *bel canto* music of the spheres;
Impressed upon the eardrums of the
Deaf (the blind would pretend, their eyeballs),
The sole figure, commonly a fugue,
To which the average aspires to
Fly. So embedded in the darkness
Like a fossil, I too entertain
Pictures of the place I want to be:

Landscape remembered as a wholly
Beloved body, here the mouth of
A river, there the foot of the hills;
An arm of the sea frames another
Neck of the woods. . . . This physical world
Abounds in arm-pits, ass-holes, navels. . . .
Bound, gagged, at the head of Death Valley
We survey a golem that distressed
Bowels of the earth did not create

Unabetted, which we may unman
By careless curiosity of
Course—illusion, if you will, and if
We will: we will, our will is in his
Peace. The creature of the air is a
Profusion, a patchwork comforter
Some in their insomnia toss off.
Which of us, survivors of ourselves,
One day will view the mayan ruin?

Whole? Herself may never hear the end
Of that ultimate *Walpurgisnacht*,
Last night, when spirits walked or flew or
Flowed to the enlightenment of flesh.
In retrospect how much might one wish
To correct or to delete! Nothing
Withstands a fanciful revision,
Yet all factual mistakes must stand
In the final draft indelible

As dawn, delectable as dream—not
That many penetrate the daylight
Stretched out cold across this crumpled sheet:
Dreams, whose cancelled versions constitute
A fair copy of experience,
Day whose lucid and pragmatic prose
Supersedes the poetry of night.
Abstract in transparent underwear
Tricks of the unconscious dissipate;

Anon, astir, my dedicated
Hosts appear for breakfast, flesh and blood—
What was I expecting? Piece by piece
We divvy up the dead body of
Our world, articulate in The Times.
Kindness in a chintzy dressing-gown
Wonders what we want to do today?
Why is this the same as everyday?
Aren't we happy just to be ourselves!

NIL NISI BONUM

O . . . the power of nothing multiplied
By infinity. Divided from us, you
Existed till they told us you had died,
Who had been the first to reject this meaningless tribute
Of mechanical verses, having tried
On the narrow tie of love, the monkey suit
Of mourning we take daily from the rack.
As for the final payment, nothing to it,
Satisfaction, and your money back,
In nearly perfect taste, the latest fashion,
Life with all its ghastly bric-a-brac.
Proverbs keep their word. On this or any occasion,
When they say nothing they mean what they say;
As they snip and cut and contrive, without party or passion,
Making to tomorrow and today
The busy fingers seldom disagree:
They are the fates, they are what people say.

BARAKAT

"Welcome, Mister, you are welcome, brother!"
  With oriental courtesy, to you
For a certain price he'd sell his mother.
  Middleman to Christian, Turk, and Jew,
Agnostic like all Greeks, or atheist,
  A shady individual who'll do
Anything, for him if it exist
  Nothing's a means and everything an end,
The world an item on a shopping list
  Whose cost depends on what you have to spend,
Dinars, dollars, pounds or pence, piastres.
  "My dear, you are at home, you are my friend."

This ikon, by the last of the Byzantine masters,
  Of the Virgin among virgins, is a pious fraud.
His faith is a lie, his victories disasters,
  His accent unlikely, his inventory odd:
Bibles, postcards, rosaries, and shells
  From the Dead Sea. He insofar resembles God,
He also manufactures what he sells,
  The secrets of all continents and seas,
Paradises, purgatories, hells. . . .

"If you believe or not, Effendi, please!
  She only need to speak, this Roman head
Of Aphrodit' "—whom eighteen centuries
  Of patina embellish. Fixed ahead,
Her empty eyes hold kindness like a vice;
  Perfection parts her lips, as if she said
Something, perhaps pronounced her asking price,
  Which naturally we cannot afford.
"Authentic reproduction! Very nice!
  A souvenir, the handmaid of the Lord—
Unusual! you will not see another
  Antique like this again, I give my word."

ACRE

The Cyclopean walls are tumbledown,
The narrow streets, dirty and confused.
The famous port washes the vacant quay
(Vacant except for dust and melon rinds)
Like dishwater: argosies of garbage
Nibbled by fish decorate the surface.

This is Acre, built by What's-His-Name,
Mentioned in the Tel Amarna tablets;
Once called, like the fishy restaurant where we ate
An Alexandrian luncheon, Ptolemais,
Then, sycophantically, Colonia Caesaris Claudii;
Fought over by the crazy crusaders, taken
By, among others, Richard Coeur de Lion,
And entered in premature triumph by an Anglican
Archbishop come all that way to see its fall.
The Teutonic Knights, of sinister memory, were started
Here. Here the Knights of St John had their hospital.

Would you like to climb the thirteenth-century tower
For a panorama of poverty-stricken streets,
Mean mosques, and, when you reach the top, the sea?
This city, which appears to have been founded by sand fleas,
Boasts the cheapest, or most comparatively inexpensive
Bazaar in the East, where the knowing traveller
May purchase at a reasonable rate
Native wares of aluminium and plastic.
Flies like tourist guides are everywhere,
The sight of the sook induces diarrhea,
Even the shopkeepers' "Welcome, Mister!" lacks the vigour
Of delivery you get in David Street.

Descend the corkscrew staircase, *Fuyons ces lieux*
Saints. Quitting the Mosque we fight our way
Out of the filthy labyrinth to the harbour,
Where the horrible children that pursued us
Hitherto are diverted by a bird,
A wounded seagull one of them has caught
By the wing, and of which they will make
First sport, then supper. Lady Hester Stanhope
Might have bought the bird and wrung its neck.
Rejecting all such missionary gestures—
Bored and itchy,who are we to judge?—
We drive away secure in our rented Hertz.

CHOUBOULOUTE

An Horatian Ode for Holly Stevens

This sand is basalt, black as a negative,
The faces too are black, also negative,
      Black pigs and cocks, black arts and beaches,
    Black as the pit or the ace of spades, black

As sin? as death? We're white as the sepulchres
One sees beside the paths, in the villages,
      With corrugated roofs and whitewashed
    Walls, where the dead are at home in blackness.

Islands attract impermanent visitors,
Requests to go back home from the residents;
      If paradise were not an island
    How could the landlord be so exclusive?

The Caribs went, and so did the Arawak
Before them, when like God the conquistador
      Came, bringing strange diseases, smallpox,
    Measles and syphilis, fatal imports;

And blacks in fact were later imported to
Supply the Créole's lack, proletariate
      To cut the sugarcane, banana,
    Pineapple, manioc, with machetes,

Or fish the crawling, dangerous Atlantique.
Their masters, who espoused the philanthropy
      That philosophes enjoined in eighteenth-
Century France, gave their cattle freedom.

Who knows where that might lead? But Napoléon,
First Consul, later Emperor, recognized
      That freedom needs a double standard.
    Joséphine Bonaparte, Empress, upstart,

Restored her fellow Créoles to slavery
As local girl made good in a fairytale.
        At last the onset of effective
    Menopause led her to Malmaison where

La Citoyenne—society's sobriquet—
Resumed her role as rose-lover. History,
        Which teaches little save statistics,
    Doesn't record if she missed her native

Savannah where today there's a monument
To this romantic schemer and courtesane
        Whose heart was Caribbean bullion,
    Practical daughter of Fort de France,

Marie Joseph Rose Tascher de la Pagerie.
Pélé's volcano muttered and fidgeted
        Until one day it had a breakdown,
    Filling the centre of Saint Pierre with

A flood of fireworks. Henceforth the capital
Of Martinique's a Mediterranean
        Provincial town, Tahitian village
    Built on the ashes of buried Paris.

La belle époque deserved a catastrophe.
Preserved in lava like Herculaneum,
        Remembered as a place of culture,
    Literature and the arts of living,

The site of 1902 has been visited.
The Arawak, a cereal, civilized
        Ceramic people first were eaten
    Up by the palaeolithic Caribs;

The French, they say, will eat almost anything
That doesn't get them first, like a fer-de-lance;
        A mongoose, though, can kill his cobra
    And is required to do so daily

In public. Any wonder a madwoman
Directed *tous les blancs* to return to our
        Pays Natal, the Riviera?
    Grande Rivière is another prospect

Entirely: the bays in the permanent
Arrest of cliffs, the swell with its permanent
        Attack upon black rocks where pastel
    Fishermen's cabins attach the tideline;

But here took place (perhaps) the penultimate
Sublime and silly romanesque episode
        Of *Paul et Virginie*, the scene where,
    Rather than take off her pants there perished

In sight of land the eponymous heroine?
Or was it off the Isle of Réunion
        That Paul and Virginie were parted,
    Innocent savages, but of colour?

Beloved Césaire preaches his negritude
To multicoloured beautiful citizens
        Of France, the heirs of Pascal, Curie,
    Diderot, Debussy, Gauguin, Schoelcher;

And we who came but brought no superior
Cuisine or language, culture or theory,
        And take away impressions, sand fleas,
    Dysentry, souvenirs, *rhum,* and sunburn,

What were we looking for in geography?
The island's shape reduced to a passenger
        From overhead the way the airplane
Abendlandsuntergang circles homeward.

OMEGA

Effaced, the unimportant hours of the day:
Three. Four. Five. Six? Seven
Again is legible, but six
In place of the vanished second hand was never
Meant to be.

As the digit that indicates the minutes
Fidgets about the still invisible six
The slower thumb thumps down upon a figure
To contradict the flibbertigibbet index
Whose interest in stability is nil.

A border of acanthus
Leaves, whose symbolism I forget,
Is worn as if by the near reiteration
Of so many identical intervals;
Worn

On the wrist or flaunted on the forearm,
What looks like a barbarian ornament
In a picture by Sir Lawrence
Alma-Tadema, the so-called master
Of the everyday antique.

When one is young one doesn't want a watch,
Depending instead on instinct or the sun.
To the moment
One said, "See you later!"
For ever, soon.

Inaccurate, old-fashioned Omega,
You tarry,
Your spring is chronically weak,
Your hands are tremulous; and yet,
Your crystal cracked, you tell the time

Not as in Moscow or Jerusalem,
Not Greenwich Meantime or Daylight Saving Time,
But time as it is meted out in Heaven,
The last letter of the alphabet
Being the initial of eternity.

LINEAR A

For James Merrill

ἕνεκα ἀοιδῆς
ἥν νέον ἕν δέλτοισιν ἐμοῖς ἐπὶ γούνασι θῆκα
Batrachomyomachia

A

In the beginning is the syllable.
The rebus-writing of the universe
Puzzles our palaeographer until
He deduces it must be [free] verse.
The vatic instinct is [in]fallible.
Be[gin or be]ing, while the wo[rk] is [te]rse
Shew]s what a demiurge is capable
Of: a sow's [ear out of a] silken purse.

B (*Delphoi*)

The curious and desperate go [too] far.
Since the [time?] of [dawn?] contemporary
Pilgrims come to the oracular
Spot where [*lacuna*] slew the serpent fairy
Teleph[one]—Parnassus bears the scar—
Like adolescents in the dictionary
Looking up a word for what they are.

Γ (*Olympia*)

Elements compose a landscape: queer
Haphazard ruins, some few handsome trees,
A hill, a sort of protozoic frieze
Where hieratic characters appear:
The [one] that follows and the [one] that flees,
[Indecent details delicately clear]
With possibly a Mourning Siren here,
And here, an Impersonation of the Breeze.

Δ (*Bassai*)

Apollo turns [his back upon] the world.
Faced with the uncomely mountainside,
No wonder he's so beautifully preserved,
Ageless [mythological] and blind.
The other immortals, who are More Than Kind,
Say it was no less than he deserved
Because of the anthropo[morphic pride
Naturally incarnate in the word].

E

"Mind of Apollo"—whatever that may be!
Glazed, hermetic as a casserole.
Know [*thyself*,] *Nothing* [*in excess*], a whole
Treatise on the single letter E:
E[very] e[mpty-day] e[piphany].
Inspiration signifies the sole
Undisputed world authority,
Inventor of cosmetics and the soul.

F

Eternal youth? Eternal [middle]age
Lies [in the gift] of the Olympians
Whose ever-during date is yesterday.
What if their make-up were [every]man's?
What would you expect [a god] to say?
A commonplace is sacred if it scans.
The Alph[abet] meanders on the page,
Spondaic as all rivers: *panta rhei*.

Z

Beneath the Epicure the silly herd
Browses on theatrically curved
Natural terraces the valley wide.
Visiting Arcadia you find
The infrastructure of the underworld
Which, hypnotized by his bucolic guide,
The [Ptolemaic] cosmonaut observed,
[Apollo out of sight and out of mind].

H (*Pylos*)

What a place to start looking for a father!
At night [the little port is full of life—
What passes [for it in the guidebook, rather.
The fort down the coast, marked with fork and knife,
Serves [heroes] roasted whole. A little farther
Out there squats the unrepentant [wife
Re]domesticated after the long [p]other
Of controversy, heavenly trouble and strife.

40

Θ (*Gytheion*)

[Once you've seen one rape you've seen them all.]
More than the noise, the smell, the dirt, the jetty,
Its customers define a port of call.
Traditionally amid a flutter of amoretti
Hence they embarqued for Asia. At landfall,
Regretfully foreseeing how the petty
Warlords she had met in her husband's hall
Would take the snub, she warned her friend [."Forget," he

I

Said, "]about the details of the trip
Arranged by Eros Tours. The naughty boy
In person is the pilot of this ship,
The hours, her deckhands, the figurehead is joy.
Ours is a bitter elixir, one sip
Of it sufficient to destroy
A civilization.["] Biting her pretty lip,
Helen fretted all the way to [Troy.

K (*Mistra*)

You were our ruin: had you withstood
The sultan another century or so,
Classical antiquity would
Have endured until today[?] As empires go,
Yours went.] But was it ever any good
After all?] itself an afterglow
Whose intensity [mis]understood
A duration [we] shall never know[?]

Λ

The Palace of the Despots on your left;
Right, the Mistress of the Universe.
[Eponymous Mistra!] bathykolpic cleft
Of Taÿgetus] superstitious nurse
Of the Renaissance; in deed, the Turk was worse.
Either [too little] or [too much] is left
Of frescoes mysteriously bereft
Of charm: Pantanassa had the curse.

M (*Mycene*)

What the cost of living must have been!
K[lytaemestra,] A[gamemnon]—tit for tat:
For all the difference between
Them, it wasn't long the royal fat
Was in the fire that licks the tablet clean.
But all the finest families come to that:
Late dynastic gold-masked king and queen
Under one stupendous beehive hat.

N (*Athens*)

Atop its wobbly acropolis,
A doll's house, Doric cheek by Roman jowl,
Immortal toy today in mortal dis-
repair, its facade disfigured by the foul
Heirs of the [X]tian metropolis
Whose modern mode of music is a howl,
The Parthenon [abandoned by Her owl?]
Grandstands above time's backward abyss.

42

Ξ

Surreptitious as a revelation,
Open-handed, [*Hydra-*]headed light
Penetrates the present; yet the sun
Is like a lover who stays out all night.
A discothèque, the beach, some shops and bars,
An architecture all of building blocks,
The absence, while it lasts, of motorcars,
The lucubrations of the native cocks [. . .]

O

Affront a uniform, push-over pilgrim
Tired, as who isn't? of his kind
Enough to make him wish to stay a week
Away from the exhaust and noise of Athens,
Looking for the original of hymn
And idyll which he somehow failed to find
Where they were so signally to seek,
Back in the [itchy] world of [aller]gens.

Π (*Ramnous*)

Puerile, to prevent a deux-chevaux
In the middle of nowhere [Her established site],
Where, while we attended rescue, night
[Gradual as Nemesis, and slow]
Overtook us, till at last the light
Expected shone, and we were free to go.
Adrastia—"inevitable"—slight
Her Nastiness, and She will let you know.

P

Who's boss? [Who pares the wants?] A dangerous,
In fact a *femme fatale*, whose promise, "Late,
But never Never!" still confounds with fuss
Who think they can control their own estate.
Providence, some times praeposterous,
At others [un]predictable as Fate,
Felicitates occasionally us.
They always serve Her turns who only wait.

Σ

From shame to [guilt, from guilt to what?] success?
Dithers our mythopoeic gyroscope
Which measures [lackaday] a little less.
How can we [un]do [ourselves un]less
Eternity provide sufficient rope?
As [whatchamacallit] slithers down the slope
Of [thingamajig], giddy amid the mess
Who think they glimpse the rusty anchor, Hope.

T

Prospects: better than they look at first.
From the sea the land seems [blank] and brown.
Turning a dull profile to the town
It shows the Mediterranean its worst,
A picture of inhospitable thirst*
That greets all comers with a Parian frown;
But just as they expect to be let down
The peripatetic pattern is reversed.

* *As Archilochus was the first to own.*

44

Υ

A microcosm: the ideal size.
Elsewhere sirens [sing] and [harpies] seize.
Exile's an untidy paradise,
Chryselephantine island, sapphire seas,
A parish visited by butterflies,
Dolphins, donkeys, pleasure-seekers, bees,
Where those who hold [our] knitting on [their] knees
Dropped a stitch in [lieu of] a surprise.

Φ

Inhuman[kindness cannot be forgiven.
Who can forgive what they don't understand?
Difficult to bear, the gifts of heaven,
Notoriously on the other hand.
Whatever god you ask, the odds are even
You will get rather more than you demand.
Welcome in the spirit they were given
The] beauties [of the god-forsaken land.

X

It is the archaeological view
That holds that [life] is short and [art] is long,
Its partisans the sometime happy few
Who know to whom the particles belong.
Yet both the ancient tongues I thought I knew
Prove in the mouth irrelevant or wrong,
And in their place I have to offer you
These *comprimés* of analgesic song.

Ψ

Here are the] tablets[. Take one a day
[Mornings before you break your fast,]
[Or bedtimes by the handful. Any way]
[The doctor orders, even first to last.]
In[decipherable pre]scription: [put away
[The pain of the present, the pleasure of the past.]
[Symptoms don't make anybody gay.]
[Set in your ways? The rule is hard and fast.]

Ω

The dippy pen when pushed to a reply:
Your drunken lover's notes are [sour] mash.
[Te]dium, te[dium], emphatically I
Take for iam[boi] anapaestic trash.
Icarus, pretender to the sky,
Ended in the water with a splash.
When hippies come to supper give them hash:
Simple, in [geo]metric terms, as π.

PHOENIX CULPA

Adam again as his namesake nude
Awoke out of the water where his sex,
Shrunken, wrinkled to a bud,
Sprung from the fork between his sapling legs.
Eve rose to meet him. Naturally blood
Flowed in reunion; flesh like artifacts
Melted. What unimaginable good—
Family ruin, innocence in rags—
Depended on their lapse they could not know.
Then how did the revolting senses guess
That in despite of death delight would grow
Immense out of proportion to distress,
Because, though the head of state had vetoed No,
Sensibly the members voted Yes?

A THOUSAND WORDS

Ce qui est beau à Leningrad, c'est Saint Petersbourg.
What fellow traveller returned from the U.S.S.R.,
Burdened with souvenirs in the form of second thoughts, said
That, rephrasing the Slavic platitude as a reactionary epigram? Thence
One must count oneself privileged to have escaped empty-handed,
Frisked in exit by the incompetent customs of the country
Who got everything backwards, inspecting my papers with a glass:
Bourgeois formalism apart, my handwriting looks like a decadent cipher.
"*Chto eto?*" The pocket epic or this wordy verse? "*Poezia.*"
Insisting it scans as prose they confiscate *War and Peace*:
The classic comeback: loved her, hated him, your eponymous warhead
In gremium qui saepe se reicit aeterno devictus vulnere amoris:
Even apologists for free love must confess this pair legally
Wed, a union no sentimental do-gooder likes to solemnize.

V., I'm afraid the authorities took away your name
Which they found in my notebook. Asked who you were,
I said, "Someone I met in a restaurant." Not so:
You were a pick-up of sorts on Nevsky Prospekt
Where as I puzzled over a plan filched from Intourist
That first evening you appeared eager to be of help.
In exchange for a few verbatim tips on English idiom
("Tell me, please, is it better, 'Here you are!' or
'There it is!' ") you afforded me a smattering of Russian—
Dom, dub, tsat, eima dvorets, knigi, mir, ya ne ponemayu,
House—oak—garden—winter-palace—books—world—I don't understand—
And your jealous services as a guide to the environs
When you were "free from class". Unlike the other touts,
Official and unofficial, who besieged the foreigners' hotel, you never
Asked for cigarettes or dollars nor offered girls or watches,
But wanted books and talk. Whether you were an agent
I am not absolute. If so, it doesn't figure.
Who sold me "art treasures" to take out, a nickel
Samovar and the biscuit bust of Pushkin, price two rubles,
From that popular Thrift Shop where one bought antiques, the

Only place in Leningrad to find silverware, glass, or china,
As department stores seemed to stock nothing but plastic gimcracks?
Enough economics—unless I just mention in passing the maids
At the hotel, patriots whom I detected to be helping
Themselves to my dwindling whisky. When I locked it up
One morning, on my return I found the bed unmade.

Still there are things I want to ask you, V.
Are you in prison or power? Were you really interrogated
As you foretold if you were seen with me? Paranoid
Melodrama I supposed, yet daily life in never-never land.
You warned me one was followed, watched, suspected, bugged, betrayed
As a matter of course, and there were certain places
We mustn't be seen together in public, like divorcées.
Out of bounds to you the doldrums of the Europa.
Every day you used to suggest some novel rendezvous
Where until you materialized no one was in evidence.

Dialectics make impossible bedfellows. Are you today the interrogator
You once were, inexhaustible in futile questions of American usage?
Following a call at the single synagogue, where we tapped
The anti-semitic party line, you invited me back for
A supper of black bread, sausage, and sweet white wine.
No English on the stair or in the common hallway
You cautioned, but your student's room itself was an asylum,
With an encyclopaedia, your father's paintings, a dusty grand piano
("I was used to play."), and the telephone. "Talk now!"
The couple embracing in the entrance, were they also spies?

What circuitous routes we pursued in our innocent sight-seeing,
How vast the meander of the stone Hermitage which holds
A pictorial history of pillaged Europe, where the fat, satisfied
Intelligent bust of the Holstein Messalina smirks from its pedestal,
As at Tsarskoe Selo, which the present regime calls Pushkin.
There, amid monumental, autumnal ruin, in a neo-gothic folly,

Lunching on lard, I learned the Russian word for cosy,
Oiutny: neither Pavlovsk, that meticulously restored memorial to filial
    resentment
Nor Peterhof's post-war proletarian Renaissance trick pavilions quite qualify.
I go on like a guidebook, there being none such.
Nowhere could we find a Russian–English, English–Russian dictionary
Or maps less rudimentary than those of a vanished century.
Lies appropriately describe this sequestrated Czarist capital founded on water,
Edifice of pure will and an idea, double-glazed window
Closed on the West. The past lingers along the Neva
Like a revisionist prince: pink, green, ochre, robin's-egg-blue
Italianate confectionery on a Scythian scale. You wanted to know
Why all foreigners are so fascinated by palaces and churches
Used as cinemas and baths? Our taste is counter-revolutionary.
Just fancy playing Soviet monopoly or enduring social-realist monotony!
And having nothing to read but Lenin and Jack London
Unless in *samizdat*! I am unable to appreciate a solitary
Line of Russian verse in translation, from Bogan to Brodski.
Although, like Leningrad at the same time fantastic and prosaic,
Your novels form a sort of exotic province of English,
I don't know why, inimitable Pushkin is a noted bore.

But who came here to talk about literature? The night
Before leaving I invited you to squander my last vouchers
Somewhere they, and we, would be accepted at face value:
After two helpings of chicken you ordered another, of veal.
Russkaya dusha! What if we were brothers? Haven't men
More in common than their wants, such as language, a
Skeleton'key rattled in so many locks? With all utopias,
The farther from perfection the better; this future that works
Looks so old-fashioned and unkind. Although the masses may
Be content, unhappy, or indifferent, excellence is an individual gesture.
Malice, too, is personal. The destroyer Aurora opposite Intourist's incongruous
Glass prison, her heroes liquidated, will she ever lift anchor
For the free world? Here, perhaps better dead than read,
Instead of the Concise Oxford Dictionary you wanted, this letter.

CHORUS

We are not citizens
But victims of the city
To which the busy joys
Of civil life commit
Us willy nilly.

Witless artisans
Or instinctive builders,
Our business bewilders
Your repulsive pity;
Our insect kingdom

Knows no unemployment,
No loyal opposition,
No leisure and no merit.
Our architecture tells you
What enjoyment

Among the denizens
Of hive and anthill is,
The energetic ethic
And collective eros of
Your spineless neighbours.

WHAT'S HIS FACE

The god that is leaving me perhaps has left
Already; bereft of his presence I breathe lighter.
What was his name? Apollo, Eros, Zeus,
As he pretends? Or one of their attendants?
By turns appalling, erotic, zoomorphic,
He might have been some petty local demon,
His divinity unrecognized by the tribe next door,
His attributes demonic to a fault,
Ithyphallic, pushy, mischievous,
Totally undependable, adept
At deceit while he denies he led you on:
Impalpable, incomprehensible . . .
He appeared in the flesh—what? half-a-dozen times?
Smiling his cryptic, unforgiving smile,
Saying little, glimpsed in intervals
Of sleep or at a distance, domestic idol
Destructive of peace and quiet. Now he's gone
Life is private again, desecrated, dull,
Without his infrequent fraudulent manifestations,
Without his unconvincing oracles.
His image, which was cast in terra cotta
And clumsily, though not unattractively, modelled,
Smashed, and his untidy shrine abandoned,
Having given nothing to his votary
Has he turned his face toward the dawn?
Is he visiting with the Hyperboreans? God
Forgive me, what made me think he was a god?

STROPHES

On the Return of Standard Time

Sodden, deadly serious,
Desperate enough to turn,
Flighty leaves assail the house.
Here are memories to burn:

Changeable fair-weather friends,
Seconds lost in paraphrase.
The long hall of Summer ends
In closed, abbreviated days

When it is time to set the clock
Back. The annual routine,
Nature's nervous tic and toc
Falters. Few and far between,

Colourful alternatives
We shall never see again,
Vegetable brief lives
Beat against the windowpane

Like the features of the dead
Materialized at a séance,
Pallid, vivid, yellow, red.
The Fall leaves everything to chance.

SWIFTS GRAB

For Marius Bewley (1916-1973)

I

Indifferent, or so we'd like to think,
To anything that might be called small change,
Such accidents of course as contradict
The circumstantial evidence of age,
Or of the age which comes to the same thing,
Whether excellent reason's or bad faith's,
It awaits alike the tardy and the swift.
Our grubby bed and breakfast is the grave,
Service compris, something next to nothing
    Nonetheless, a poor thing to have made.

II

Entranced at your unattended entrance:
If this is heaven that must be the sun,
Conspiracies of cloud before whose face
Cannot but make of coruscating, dull
Colonel West an interesting orange
Criss-crossed by circuitous arteries of
Blood or thunder; remarkable his range,
His visage that of our triumphant bull
Who when it comes to evening and age
    Owes *la douleureuse*' untidy sum.

III

Indulgent to your word, compassion for
Animals who always are mistreated
Need ulcerate your needy heart no longer.
Sub- or super- or just human weakness,
Evitable, inexcusable wrong,
The necessity of spelling evil,
Leave you extraordinarily bored.
Gourmand at the picnic of unreason,
Whatever possessed you to beg for more,
    Civil indignation, or mere pique?

54

IV

Queer lover, lady-killer, misanthrope,
In the changing room of odd and even
Twin half-spinsters adrift in the same boat,
One of them gentle, both of them simple,
Giggle each other their translated joke:
Identical in name, divorced by nature,
Stella, genealogically loath,
Vanessa, Erudition's errant daughter:
When men proclaim a woman's tongue a toast
    Let none forget the book of Esther.

V

To your so unsentimental sister
The clouds are apt to make reflections too
In that grand withdrawing-room, the sky. Her
Character (might one add, you gave her two?)
Swiftly grown more virtuous or wiser,
She calls it witty to be rude—*et tu*?
When an extra enters do you rise, Sir,
Or play stink-finger in your neighbour's stew?
Of qualities no coxcomb need be miser.
    Heaven knows what wit is coming to!

VI

The eighteenth century knew how to live,
The nineteenth how to die, the twentieth
Neither, nor does it comprehend evil
As shall we say the seventeenth did death,
But like the mediaevals draws the veil
Of sophistry across the face of faith.
Only our contemporaries are vile—
The waste! the shame! then the expense of breath!
Simulated if obscene, the act is live,
    Or so uninspired scripture saith.

VII

O Carolan, almost anonymous
Old-Irish bard, in what anthology
Shall I seek your pieces? Inglorious,
Blind, homeless, wlonk beneath a laughing sea
Of platitude, or truth? Preposterous
Oblivion your anniversary
Fee, received for drink, mere *vocis flatus*
Unmultiplied beyond necessity;
Venerable beginner, *vincibilis*
    Dodo lost in any ministrelsy.

VIII

The crossed, the busted, the ununderstood,
And who suffer anagogic symptoms,
Ecstasy, liquefaction of the blood,
Inexplicable dread, lack of balance,
With such abrupt anomalies of mood,
Impotent, awful anger such as Samson's,
That vatic frenzy that passes for wood,
Know that all these nonsenses are reasons,
Even their God whom men pronounce so good
    Relatively coins, kidnaps, cozens.

IX

Victim, if you please, of our disorder,
The orang-utan Jonathan at play
With inedible bits of silver paper
We watched at Phoenix Park the other day
Frig himself, caracol, frisk and caper,
Entertainment for a hobbledehoy,
Moves me more than may be sane or proper
To tears there is no hand to dry for aye
Flowing through unintelligible order
    Like a river, like the Milky Way.

VOWEL MOVEMENTS

Take a statement, the same as yesterday's dictation:
    Lately pain has been there waiting when I awake.
Creative despair and failure have made their patient.
    Anyway, I'm afraid I have nothing to say.
Those crazy phrases I desecrated the paper
    With against the grain . . . Taste has turned away her face
Temporarily, like a hasty, ill-paid waitress
    At table, barely capable but very vague.
Mistaken praise and blame degrade profane and sacred
    Places so strange you may not even know their names.
Vacant the gymnasium where words once played naked
    Amazing games that always used to end in mate.

Better, then, the effort than preterite perfection,
    I guess. Indeed, I envy the eminent dead
The special effects I am ready to inherit
    Less than their sentiments and impenitent sense
Of aesthetic gesture. Unpleasant and pretentious,
    The Western hemisphere has plenty to forget.
The mess men might yet make of themselves, given present
    Events! Are many content to accept the best?
Precious as sex is, flesh, perenially wretched,
    Begs the bread of heaven, blessing nevertheless
The unexpected sender's address on a letter.
    Every breathless sentence says not yet to death.

The past cannot matter except as an abstraction,
    A flattering caricature of happy lands
Wherein many a grand, imaginary castle
    In fact turns out to be a tourist trap at last,
A vast palace that adrastic phantoms inhabit.
    Maps of madness, characteristically blank,
Ask vatic questions, exact a magic answer:
    The family photograph album at a glance,
Granny, Dad, Aunt Sally, that dissatisfied madame

Who manages passion's incalculable acts,
Paris, everyman's romantic trash and tarry—
Abracadabra, and the vanished cast comes back!

If civilization isn't a silly gimmick,
    Is it the wit to wish, the will to make it stick?
The mathematical vision which built this system
    Figures the width of a minute within an inch.
Primitive physics, a sophisticated fiction,
    Insists that in principle everything is fixed.
Visitors picnic amid pretty *Chichèn Itzá*
    With its sacrificial pit, artificial hills
And cricket pitch wherein the winner is the victim.
    To think an instinct like iniquity exists!
Hidden riches fill big individual middens;
    In the Wizard's Pyramid little lizards live.

Specious sweets we reach for eagerly with Eve's evil
    Greed recede like the fleeting details of a dream.
It seems that we have been a brief season in Eden:
    Chic unreal estates where immediately green
Trees repeated in completely meaningless series
    Briefly yield to the weaker tyranny of weeds
Even as we seek relief in a secret clearing.
    Prehistory can be too recent; need we read
These steles' queried speech? Here undefeated peoples
    Experienced deceit; here scenes of deepest grief
Teach us to weep the cheap and easy tears of reason;
    Here the sea of being sleeps, a period peace.

Frustration, fuss, and lust are love's unlucky colours.
    Thunderstruck, the muscular monuments look dumb.
Judged by the numbers that once flourished in the jungle
    In hundreds of miles of dull undercover scrub,
Unless somebody was insufferably ugly
    Mistrust of one another must be in the blood.
Unsuccess in a dozen tough struggles instructs us
    Justice is a mother-fucker. Suffering's fun
For a month, but in a millenium no wonder

One becomes somewhat disgusted. Unsubtle skull,
The mysteries of dust are nothing to live up to.
    Insulted by a touch, one mutters, "Summer sucks."

Undone by the siesta and by sudden showers,
    Is it uncomfortable in the hungry South?
Now cowed by Kulkulkan's geometrical scowl,
    Now wowed by the classic brown faces in a crowd,
You falter at mounds memorial to a thousand
    Bleeding hearts in a single holiday cut out,
Submitted to the sun, insatiable flesh-flower
    Of the universe, all-devouring powerhouse,
Confounded by our sound of pronounceable vowels.
    Myths, as the guidebook says, are handed down by mouth.
Though mood and voice and person, gender, tense, and number
    Predicate a verb, its cases explain a noun:

Proper noun or pronoun, indubitably human,
    Whose beautiful excuse is usually youth
Doomed to the brutal usufructu of the future,
    Consumed by the illusions of jejune amours.
You used to choose the rules with superfluous humour,
    Tuned to the influential movements of the moon
Whose smooth, translucent route through roofless rooms illumines
    From dewy moonrise unto lunar afternoon
Tulum and its improvements, tumulus and ruins,
    Poorly reproduced, a too crudely stupid view.
Who knew nude truth from rumour, amusement from music
    Soon would prove a fool. Beauty, useless, is a wound.

On and off; the impossible is honour's motto,
    Monotony the awful drawback of my song.
What was lost was often all we had got in common,
    Our quasi-comic quandary depended on
Qu'en dirai-je? chronic, colossal hypochondry,

Neurotic complication or hypnotic calm.
Gods begotten of loss, not bronze nor terra cotta,
    Haunt the province of law, of cause and conscious wrong.
Following the Long Count a lot has been forgotten:
    Positive nonsense, fraud, false plots and hollow talk,
Soporific concepts toppled by fall or conquest,
    The cosmos as a model watch that wants to stop.

At any moment the doors of the soul may open
    And those reproachful ghosts invoked from the remote
Coasts of tomorrow begin to impose the order
    Of bone and trophy, home and the odour of smoke.
O mornings that broke on the slopes of cold volcanos,
    Almost frozen, golden and old-rose, like a scroll
Slowly unfolded, or a brocade robe thrown over
    The throne of the mountains, cloaking their cones in snow!
Hope, an emotion swollen by every omen,
    No psychotrope, only a semiprecious stone,
Topaz or opal, adorns the close of the strophe.
    Woe wrote these notes in a code also known as prose.

Ode: this leafy, streamless land where coy waters loiter
    Under the embroidered soil, subterfluous coin
Of another culture destroyed by lack of moisture,
    Spoiled by the unavoidable poison of choice.
Archaeological lawyers exploit the foibles
    Of a royalty that in time joined *hoi polloi*:
History's unemployed, geography's anointed,
    Unlike the orchids of the forests, spin and toil.
Imperfectly convinced of final disappointment,
    Persuaded of the possibility of joy,
Pen poised for the pointless impressions of those voices
    That boil up like bubbles on the face of the void,

Finally I try to define why divine silence
    Underlies the tidy designs of paradise.
Priceless as the insights of the inspired psyche,
    Blind, violent as a geyser, right as a rhyme,
Fine ideas likely to undermine the idle
    Mind divided between the types of fire and ice,
"Highly stylized" politely describes the bright eyesores
    Shining like diamonds or rhinestones in the night sky,
Lifelike, provided life survives its vital cycle
    And the tireless indictment of time's diatribe,
While mankind, sightless, frightened, like a child in twilight,
    Dies of the devices it was enlightened by.

    Amazing games that always used to end in mate!
Precious as sex is, flesh, perennially wretched,
    In fact turns out to be a tourist trap at last.
The mathematical vision which built this system
    Of the universe, all-devouring powerhouse,
(The mysteries of dust are nothing to live up to!)
    Briefly yields to the weaker tyranny of weeds.
You used to choose the rules with superfluous humour:
    Monotony, the awful drawback of my song,
Slowly unfolded, like a brocade robe thrown over.
    Persuaded of the possibility of joy,
Finally I tried to define why divine silence . . .

LETTER TO SHADOW

Bit by bit, as in a picture puzzle,
    The prospect of this present disappears
Into that panorama of the past.
    Dotted with illegible menhirs
The flat and sentimental landscape that
    You read as a romance, the prose plateau
Of fancy half-developed like a snapshot
    Lies printed with the alphabet of shadow.

From left to right, an amphisbaenic sense,
    Black on white, a sensuous photograph
Of a too formal period, death's sentence
    Closing life's emotional paragraph,
Tuneless, tasteless, without text or tincture,
    (N.B., hieroglyphics have no tenses)
Lucid and superficial cynosure,
    Literature is all a letter says.

What alternative to tell a vision?
    So doting on the idiotical light
Within's like staring at the sun: one
    Sees no more than if he looked at midnight . . .
Midday composes shortest, sharpest shade,
    Underlining objects in italics
On our universal page whose man-made
    Margins a little intuition fix

In the dictionary mirror.
    Seeing if you nab one you feel nothing,
Imitation, neither less nor more,
    Its shadow is the name of anything,
The mystery whereby sight were baffled,
    Sacrament and written character,
Labarum above the battlefield
    Of words, which always was a massacre.

DARYL HINE

Daryl Hine was born in British Columbia, Canada, in 1936. He studied Classics and Philosophy at McGill University in Montreal. He then lived principally in France until 1962, when he returned to this continent, first, briefly to New York, and then, in 1963, to the University of Chicago, where he resumed his studies, taking a Ph.D. in comparative literature in 1967. The subject of his doctoral thesis was the Latin poetry of George Buchanan, the sixteenth-century Scottish humanist. He has taught at the University of Chicago, Northwestern University and the University of Illinois, and is the editor of *Poetry* magazine.